Blue Ribbon Animals

SHOWING CHICKENS AT THE FAIR

 Gareth Stevens
PUBLISHING

By Jennifer Wendt

Please visit our website, www.garethstevens.com. For a free color catalog of all our high-quality books, call toll free 1-800-542-2595 or fax 1-877-542-2596.

Cataloging-in-Publication Data

Names: Wendt, Jennifer.
Title: Showing chickens at the fair / Jennifer Wendt.
Description: New York : Gareth Stevens Publishing, 2019. | Series: Blue ribbon animals | Includes glossary and index.
Identifiers: ISBN 9781538232842 (pbk.) | ISBN 9781538229279 (library bound) | ISBN 9781538232859 (6pack)
Subjects: LCSH: Chickens--Juvenile literature. | Chickens--Life cycles--Juvenile literature.
Classification: LCC SF487.5 W46 2019 | DDC 636.5--dc23

First Edition

Published in 2019 by
Gareth Stevens Publishing
111 East 14th Street, Suite 349
New York, NY 10003

Copyright © 2019 Gareth Stevens Publishing

Designer: Katelyn E. Reynolds
Editor: Emily Mahoney

Photo credits: Cover, p. 1 (chicken) Valentina_S/Shutterstock.com; cover, p. 1 (background photo) chainarong06/Shutterstock.com; cover, p. 1 (blue banner) Kmannn/Shutterstock.com; cover, pp. 1-24 (wood texture) Flas100/Shutterstock.com; pp. 2-24 (paper) Peter Kotoff/Shutterstock.com; p. 4 Tsekhmister/Shutterstock.com; p. 5 TierneyMJ/Shutterstock.com; p. 7 (Polish) Teresa Otto/Shutterstock.com; p. 7 (Rhode Island Red) Natalia Paklina/Shutterstock.com; p. 7 (Dominique) Muskoka Stock Photos/Shutterstock.com; p. 7 (Brahma) Ciobaniuc Adrian Eugen/Shutterstock.com; p. 7 (Dutch Bantam) Igor Grochev/Shutterstock.com; p. 7 (Cochin) M Rutherford/Shutterstock.com; p. 9 Omjai Chalard/Shutterstock.com; p. 11 Image Source/Getty Images; p. 13 Sollina Images/Blend Images/Getty Images; p. 15 © 2011 Dorann Weber/Moment Open/Getty Images; p. 16 Iryna Liveoak/Shutterstock.com; p. 17 Laura Stone/Shutterstock.com; p. 19 joyfuldesigns/Shutterstock.com; p. 21 Adrian Samson/Photodisc/Getty Images.

Printed in the United States of America

CPSIA compliance information: Batch #CW19GS: For further information contact Gareth Stevens, New York, New York at 1-800-542-2595.

CONTENTS

Words in the glossary appear in **bold** type the first time they are used in the text.

CHICKENS AT THE FAIR

Showing animals at the fair, or making them look their best to be judged, is a fun **experience.** It's also a lot of work! One of the animals you can choose to show at the fair may surprise you.

It has feathers, a beak, and lays eggs. If you guessed it's a chicken, you're right! Read on to learn how to take home a blue ribbon at the fair by showing your chicken.

Raising chickens and showing them at the fair is fun!

5

PICKING YOUR CHICKEN

If you want to show a chicken at the fair, you'll first need to get a chicken. Read about different **breeds** before making your choice. You'll also need to decide if you want to show a hen (a female chicken) or a rooster (a male chicken).

If you don't already have chickens, you can go to a local farm store or search the internet to find a local farm. You'll want to pick a young chick so you can start to train them right away.

These are some popular breeds of chickens that are shown at fairs.

POLISH

RHODE ISLAND RED

DOMINIQUE

BRAHMA

DUTCH BANTAM

COCHIN

CARING FOR YOUR CHICKEN

Part of raising a chicken to show at the fair is being **responsible** for its care. Your chicken will need a warm, safe place to live while it's growing. It needs a **coop** or pen large enough for it to get some exercise. You'll need to clean your chicken's **bedding** daily.

Chickens grow very fast. You'll want to feed your chicken a healthy **diet.** Ask your **veterinarian** what the best food is for your type of chicken.

TAKE THE PRIZE!

DID YOU KNOW THAT TOO MUCH SUN WILL FADE YOUR CHICKEN'S FEATHERS?

Chicks need plenty of clean water and food to become blue-ribbon winners.

WORKING WITH YOUR CHICKEN

The more you work with your chicken, the better you'll both do at the fair. Practice gently picking up your young chick and holding it. You can also have a friend or family member gently pick it up and hold it so it gets used to being around other people.

Practice taking your chicken out of its pen headfirst. Place one hand over its back and your other hand under its body. Gently hold its legs. This is how you'll handle your chicken at the fair.

COMB

BEAK

EYE

TAIL

WATTLE

WING

FEET

PREPARING FOR THE FAIR

Keeping your chicken healthy is important. Read the rules for your fair and make sure your chicken has had all the **vaccinations** and blood tests it needs to be able to compete at the fair. Keep the records so you can show the fair **officials.**

A few weeks before the fair, practice moving your chicken in and out of its exhibit coop. You'll do this in front of the judge at the fair. Be sure the coop is large enough for your chicken's food and water.

TAKE THE PRIZE!

STUDY YOUR FAIR GUIDE TO LEARN WHAT THE JUDGES WILL BE LOOKING AT FOR YOUR TYPE OF CHICKEN.

When taking your chicken out of its coop, handle it gently so you don't break its feathers.

13

GROOMING YOUR CHICKEN

A few days before the fair, you'll want to give your chicken a bath. Dip your chicken in warm water with some gentle shampoo, wipe gently, and then rinse. Dry your chicken carefully with a towel. It can take at least a day for your chicken to dry completely.

A toothbrush works great for cleaning your chicken's feet. Some people use baby oil to make their chicken's feet shine. Depending on your chicken's breed, you can use a comb or brush to fluff its feathers.

TAKE THE PRIZE!

YOU CAN KEEP YOUR SUPPLIES IN A TOOLBOX. BE SURE TO INCLUDE: A TOWEL, A WASHTUB, GENTLE SHAMPOO, A COMB OR BRUSH, A TOOTHBRUSH, AND A NAIL FILE.

Practice giving your chicken a bath a few weeks before the fair so it isn't **stressed** before the show.

15

AT THE FAIR

It's time to go to the fair! Check in with fair officials to find out where you'll be keeping your chicken. Write your name and your chicken's information on a special coop tag. The judges will be looking at this.

Keep the coop clean and check on your chicken often to make sure it has fresh water and food. Use your own buckets and scoops from home to water and feed your chicken. Sometimes other chickens can carry **viruses**.

When you arrive at the fair, check in and take your chicken to its **temporary** coop.

SHOWING YOUR CHICKEN

When you check in at the fair, you'll be given a time to show your chicken. Be on time! Clean your chicken's coop and do a quick wipedown of your chicken right before you take it to the show area.

You'll want to look your best, too! Wear a clean shirt and pants and keep your hair neat. You may have to answer simple questions about your chicken. What does it eat? How old is it? What breed of chicken is it?

TAKE THE PRIZE!

IT'S IMPORTANT TO LEARN ABOUT THE PARTS OF A CHICKEN. THE JUDGE MAY ASK YOU TO NAME AND POINT OUT CERTAIN PARTS OF YOUR CHICKEN TO THEM.

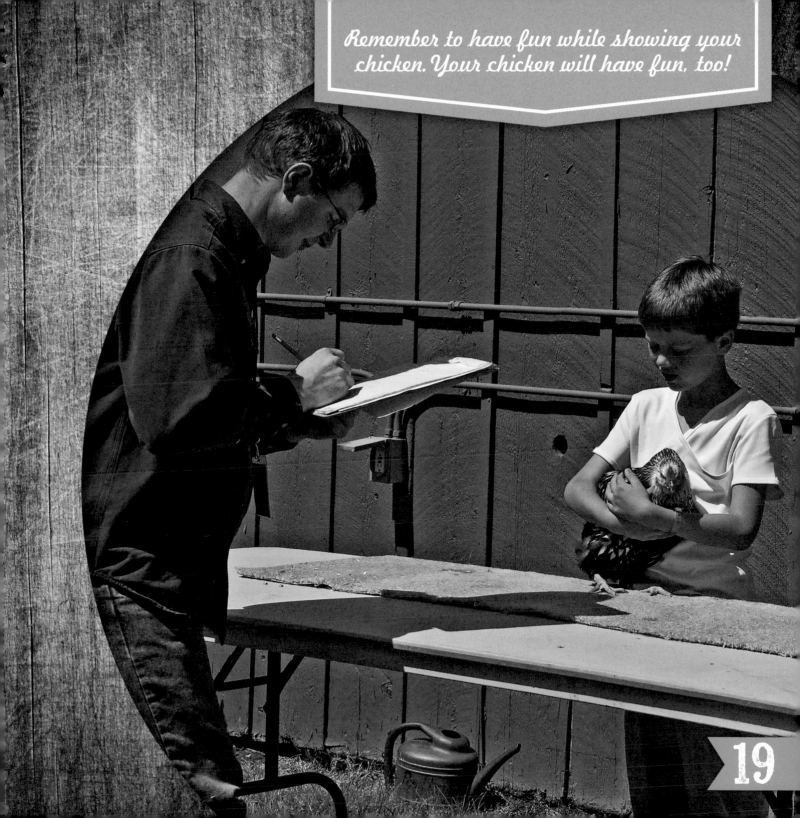

Remember to have fun while showing your chicken. Your chicken will have fun, too!

19

AFTER THE FAIR

Hopefully your hard work earns you and your chicken a blue ribbon! Not everyone wins a blue ribbon, but by showing your chicken at the fair you get to meet new people, learn more about your animal, and gain skills to help you at the next fair.

Remember to clean up your area when the fair is over. Gather your supplies and don't leave a mess. Be sure to thank everyone who has helped you take care of your chicken during the fair.

TAKE THE PRIZE!

YOU MAY HAVE TO **QUARANTINE** YOUR CHICKEN FOR A WHILE WHEN YOU TAKE IT HOME. IT MAY HAVE PICKED UP A VIRUS FROM BEING AROUND OTHER CHICKENS, AND IT COULD MAKE YOUR OTHER ANIMALS AT HOME SICK.

Winning a ribbon is great, but the experience of raising a chicken and showing it is even better!

21

GLOSSARY

bedding: matter used for an animal's bed, such as straw, newspaper, or wood shavings

breed: a group of animals that share features different from other groups of the kind

coop: a small building where chickens are kept

diet: the food an animal eats

experience: something that you have done or that has happened to you

official: a person who has a position of authority in a company, organization, or government

quarantine: to keep a person or animal away from others to stop the spread of an illness

responsible: having the job or duty of dealing with or taking care of something or someone

stressed: feeling worried, concerned, or nervous

temporary: lasting for a limited time

vaccination: a shot that keeps a person or animal from getting a certain sickness

veterinarian: a doctor who is trained to treat animals

virus: a very tiny thing that can cause illness when it enters the body

For More Information

BOOKS

Murray, Julie. *Chickens*. Minneapolis, MN: Abdo Kids, 2016.

Reynolds, Shaye. *The Life Cycle of a Chicken*. New York, NY: PowerKids Press, 2016.

WEBSITES

Chickens
www.dkfindout.com/us/animals-and-nature/domesticated-animals/chickens/
Learn more about chickens and watch a video about chicken facts.

4-H
4-h.org
4-H gives children a chance to learn new skills through hands-on projects.

National FFA Organization
www.ffa.org
Future Farmers of America is an education-based organization for students interested in farming.

INDEX